Printed in Great Britain
by Amazon

26012332R00071